Public Lending Right
Annual Report and
Account 2005-2006

Ordered by the House of Commons
to be printed 19 July 2006

Report, by the Secretary of State for Culture,
Media and Sport, on the PLR Scheme 2005-06,
incorporating the Registrar's Annual Review,
presented to Parliament pursuant to Section 3(8)
of the Public Lending Right Act 1979;
Account, of the Public Lending Right Central
Fund, presented to Parliament pursuant
to Section 2(6) of the PLR Act 1979, for the
year ended 31 March 2006.

HC 1372 LONDON: The Stationery Office £11.10

The images in this year's Report feature Seven Stories, the Centre for Children's Books. Located in Newcastle-upon-Tyne, the Centre collects, explores and exhibits original manuscripts and artwork by British writers and illustrators for children.

In its celebration of children's books it fits well with the themes running through this year's PLR Report. PLR plays a vital role in supporting the work of the country's writers, illustrators, editors and translators who make such important individual contributions to the wider UK creative economy and to Britain's pre-eminence in fields such as children's literature.

PLR is very grateful to Seven Stories, and to the authors and illustrators whose work is featured, for permission to reproduce this material in the Report. In addition, PLR is pleased to acknowledge the co-operation and enthusiasm of the staff and pupils from Grange Park Primary (Year 6) and South Beach First School (Year 1).

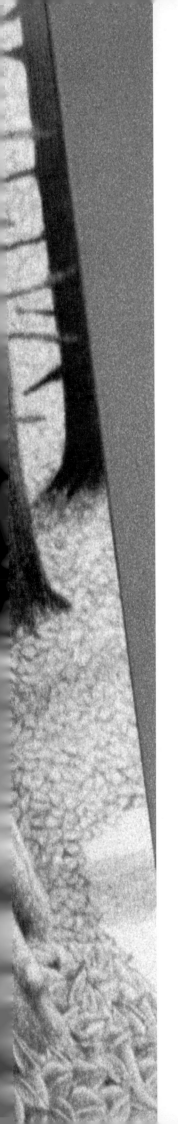

Report on the
**Public Lending Right
Scheme** and Account
2005-2006

Cover: JK Rowling's illustration and hand-written drafts for *Harry Potter and the Philosopher's Stone*, part of the Incredible Journeys exhibition. Frontispiece: exterior of the Seven Stories building.

Title page: Illustration ©2004 Anthony Browne. From the front cover of *Into the Forest* by Anthony Browne. Reproduced by permission of Walker Books Ltd, London SE11 5HJ. The image was used in his design for the Dark Dark Woods section of Incredible Journeys.

Registrar's Annual Review: the Book Den

Scheme Developments: Illustrations © 1999 Helen Oxenbury From *Alice's Adventures in Wonderland* by Lewis Carroll, illustrated by Helen Oxenbury Reproduced by permission of Walker Books Ltd, London SE11 5HJ. Exhibit in Incredible Journeys

Page 45: Image from *The Gruffalo* written by Julia Donaldson, illustrated by Axel Scheffler (© 1999 Macmillan Children's Books, Macmillan Publishers Limited)

Guest Features: The Story Catcher workshop in the Artist's Attic.

Pages 66-67: detail from the original typescript for *The Borrowers* by Mary Norton.

End Page: hand-written note from the Faith Jaques collection.

Design and art direction by Antman
Photography by Steve Benbow
Scanning by Peninsular Services
Printing and finishing by Maslands

Contents

Preface
The Secretary of State for Culture, Media and Sport

Registrar's Annual Review

Scheme Developments

Guest Feature

PLR Central Fund Account 2005-06

Preface

I am very pleased to lay before Parliament this Report by the Registrar of Public Lending Right on the operation of the PLR Scheme 2005-06.

PLR, first recognised in legislation in 1979 after many years of campaigning by authors, ensures that they are remunerated by the government for the free lending out of their books by public libraries. It is now a well established right enjoying widespread recognition for the key role it plays in supporting the literary endeavours of the country's authors on which so much of the creative economy depends. I am delighted that so many writers, illustrators, editors and translators are benefiting from the PLR Scheme and it is very encouraging to read in the Report examples of the very positive feedback that the Registrar and his team receive from authors on their management of the Scheme. The benefits of PLR are now recognised internationally and increasingly the experience of the UK's PLR team is being called upon to help with the start up of new schemes in other parts of Europe. Three of these schemes are now making PLR payments to UK authors as well as to their own.

The Registrar and his team have been successful in meeting the challenging targets that my Department agreed with them for the running costs of the Scheme, thus enabling them to distribute a record level of payments to over 18,500 authors in February this year. This is against a background of continued expansion in the number of authors registering for PLR, and in the number of library authorities participating in PLR's library sample.

The Registrar reports the successful completion of projects to automate the calculation and recording of payments to authors, and to introduce an electronic records management system developed by PLR's own in-house IT team. The on-line registration system introduced last year for authors continues to grow in popularity with 50% of registrations now taking place this way, and I look forward to hearing of the planned next stage of this initiative which will enable authors to have more direct access to the information held on the PLR database. I would like to thank Jim Parker and his team for administering the Scheme so efficiently, and to congratulate him on his reappointment as Registrar for a further five years from August 2006.

I am also grateful for the work of the PLR Advisory Committee which, under the chairmanship of Simon Brett, continues to provide my Department with excellent advice on the operation of the Scheme and on its future direction.

The Rt Hon Tessa Jowell MP
Secretary of State for Culture, Media and Sport

Registrar's Overview

This Report is primarily concerned with describing our work over the last year in administering the PLR Scheme in line with our statutory responsibilities. We aim to do this efficiently, cost-effectively and fairly, with the emphasis on providing authors with the best service possible. The Scheme works to an annual cycle of registering new authors and books, collecting and processing loans data from the public library authorities in our statistical sample, and calculating and distributing payments. In 2005-06 we agreed a number of key performance measures with DCMS, and our success in meeting these is described in the Report.

Our key target for the year was to hold running costs to the level agreed with DCMS in our Funding Agreement. We achieved our target enabling us to distribute £6.54 million in author payments. The Scheme continues to grow annually with the total number of registered authors now standing at 36,000. Last year saw the highest increase in registrations at 1,400. Contributing to this growth have been our successful promotion of the Scheme in the UK and Europe, and the accessibility of the on-line registration system.

PLR does not operate in isolation; there are many strands that link us to developments in related sectors. These include the modernization of our processes, principally ICT developed in support of the wider e-government agenda; the contribution PLR makes to the country's creative economy by supporting authors' livelihoods; enhanced electronic accessibility to our unique data for the public library community; and our leading role in supporting the spread of PLR across Europe.

One of the year's major challenges has been the conversion of our systems to cope with the new 13 digit ISBN format. Our in-house IT team have also modified and modernized our systems to enhance the way we manage the Scheme and to improve accessibility for authors and libraries. We completed the automation of author payment records, and implemented phase one of our electronic records management system as well as continuing to develop e-registration. Work has continued on the LEWIS service; this will make our unique database of book loans information accessible to a wider audience. It has been developed with the needs of libraries in mind and we look forward to running a pilot with seven library authorities in the coming year. To build on these successes we have also begun with the Advisory Committee a wider review of the Scheme's operation to help us identify further scope for efficiencies.

The government is increasingly recognizing the economic value of the creative industries and the contribution of individual creators is crucial here. In our own sector the output of writers, illustrators, translators, editors and other contributors to published works is essential to the success of publishing and related industries. We may be one of DCMS's smallest sponsored bodies but the impact of our work is far reaching. As well as the direct financial support that PLR provides, authors often cite the psychological importance of the link we create to their library readership. Authors repeatedly mention this in the regular surveys we undertake to gauge their views on the Scheme's operation.

PLR also plays an active role in supporting national initiatives to improve and develop public libraries through partnerships with organizations such as The Reading Agency, the Arts Council and the Museums, Libraries and Archives Council. PLR loans data is now widely used to support reader development and stock promotions and to help chart their success.

Activity in the European Community has been another major part of our work. The 1992 EU Lending Right Directive requires all 25 member states to establish a PLR system. We have run a series of best practice seminars as the Directive is rolled out across Europe. Six years ago we took the pioneering decision to open our own PLR Scheme to authors living in all EU states. Three member states now reciprocate paying PLR to UK authors from their schemes.

The Registrar's Team
The Registrar is supported by Sue Ridge, his PA. Evelyn Relph, Assistant Registrar, is responsible to the Registrar for the day-to-day running of PLR; Julia Coxon, Project and Communications Specialist, reports to the Assistant Registrar.

Incredible Journeys exhibition: JK Rowling's illustration and drafts for *Harry Potter and the Philosopher's Stone*

Table 1
Two Year Comparison
2004/05 - 2005/06

Payment Date	22nd year Feb 2005	23rd year Feb 2006
Expenditure		
Government Funding	£7,381,000	£7,419,000
Operating Costs	£812,000	£822,000
Payments to Authors (to nearest 10,000)	£6,540,000	£6,540,000
Rate Per Loan	5.26p	5.57p
Authors' Earnings		
£6,000	285	281
£5,000 - £5,999.99	70	68
£2,500 - £4,999.99	376	390
£1,000 - £2,499.99	783	782
£500 - £999.99	911	959
£100 - £499.99	3,826	3,725
£5 - £99.99	12,415	12,379
Total Recipients	18,666	18,584
Registrations		
Total Book 'Interests' (to date)	383,042	402,835
'Interests' Registered to 'New' Authors	3,755	4,577
'Interests' Registered to 'Old' Authors	12,327	15,196
Sample Book Loans		
Total UK Loans	361m	341m
Loans Sampled by PLR	71m	78m
(As % of UK Loans)	20%	23%
Registered Loans (estimated)	158m	148m
(As % of UK Loans)	44%	44%

PLR's full audited accounts
These are prepared on an accruals basis
[see pp 75 to 97]. The summary figures
above are expressed in cash terms and
rounded off.

Stairwell serving the seven floors of Seven Stories. It is said that there are only seven stories in fiction.

Registration

Objective 1
All new authors and books were registered by the 30 June 2005 deadline, including 1,406 authors registering for the first time.

Objective 2
We aimed to achieve a 95% satisfaction rate from authors consulted on the service provided by PLR. (99% achieved.)

Author Services Team

Author Services Manager, Carolyn Gray, manages this busy department with its team of six people. They are responsible for looking after 36,000 registered authors and for collecting loans data from the 38 library authorities across the UK which make up the PLR sample. Here Carolyn Gray gives her overview of the year.

Author and Book Registration

It's been an exceptionally busy year with a record number of new authors and other rightsholders applying for PLR registration: 1,400 in total. 7,000 book applications were submitted and processed between July 2004 and June 2005. The team works hard to give authors and rightsholders the best possible service, dealing with applications and enquiries promptly and efficiently. Our aim is to achieve service satisfaction levels in excess of 95%. I'm delighted that we achieved an impressive figure of 99% this year, with 65% of authors rating the service as 'excellent'.

Here are just a few of the comments.
"I was very impressed when, during a meeting, my accountant had cause to phone through to one of your staff members with a question which was answered promptly, professionally and profitably. If only other bodies could operate with such friendly efficiency!"
"It is an excellent service: very prompt, reliable and courteous."
"Your staff are very friendly and helpful."

Ethnic Monitoring

An important strand of our work has been the analysis of a recent survey of the ethnic backgrounds of authors applying for PLR. The analysis will help us target specific groups of writers to ensure that the ethnic diversity of our registered authors is representative of the national picture. We are in the process of developing our promotional plans for the coming year.

On-Line Registration

Authors are generally very happy with the on-line registration service and around half of all book applications processed were submitted electronically. We have followed up a number of authors' suggestions which have included e-mailing news updates and reminders of key dates. Judging by the response, it was clear that our mail-out to remind authors of the closing date for book registration was much appreciated and we will repeat this next year.

The year saw the completion of vital work on PLR's author payments and document management systems. The challenge for the team in the coming year will be to get the next stage of the on-line registration system developed. Authors are very keen to check their book details and payment statements on-line. In response to authors' comments and suggestions a list of development options has been drawn up and work has already started.

Loans Data Collection

The other main responsibility for the Author Services team is the selection of sample library authorities and the collection and checking of the loans data transmitted to us. This is the data used to calculate payments to authors.

Objective 3
All loans data from the 2004–05 library sample was received and processed by the 30 June 2005 deadline; as planned, we rotated the composition of the sample introducing ten new authorities from 1 July 2005 increasing the sample size to 39 authorities.

The Library Sample
Loans information for the February 2006 payments came from 38 authorities, including data from over 1,000 service points and covering the year July 2004 to June 2005. At 23% this was the highest percentage of UK loans data processed to date. Our goal is to ensure all this data is processed accurately and on schedule for the annual payment calculations prior to distribution each February.

In July 2005, 10 new authorities joined the scheme, increasing the sample to a record 39 authorities. From July 2006 it increases to 41 authorities. This is in line with plans to expand the size and improve the fairness of the sample.

Objective 4
We aimed to achieve a satisfaction rate of 95% from sample library authorities consulted on the service provided by PLR. (98% achieved.)

Our service target was to achieve a 95% satisfaction rate from sample library authorities; we exceeded this with a figure of 98%.

ISBN-13
A major challenge this year has been the work to ensure a smooth changeover from the 10 digit to 13 digit ISBN which has to be achieved by January 2007. It is vital that PLR's computer system and those of its partner organisations are able to operate with the new format. For PLR, this means a virtual rewrite of the entire registration and loans data systems. With our IT team we are on schedule with this development work and are in regular contact with library management system and bibliographic suppliers to ensure their systems will also be ready. As some libraries are already processing a

small number of loans for books with 13 digit ISBNs, we are using an in-house system that converts the ISBN to its original 10 digit format so that authors do not lose out on any loans. We aim to have completed the system redesign by October 2006 when we will convert all ISBNs to 13 digits.

Author Services Manager, Carolyn Gray is supported by Joanne Gayford, Registration Specialist, with Kelly Bowstead and Claire Balmer as Registration Officers; Janice Forbes, European Specialist, and Sarah Beamson, Library Specialist, with Paul Atkinson as Library Officer.

A corner of the Book Den

Table 2
Sample Library Authorities
2004/05 and 2005/06

England

Bedfordshire/Luton*	Kent	Lancashire*
Buckinghamshire/Milton Keynes	Derbyshire/Derby	Stoke-on-Trent
Devon*	Northumberland	West Sussex
Nottinghamshire/Nottingham	Hampshire	Worcestershire
Windsor & Maidenhead		

Metropolitan Districts

Coventry	Bolton	Leeds*
The Wirral	North Tyneside	

Greater London Boroughs

Brent	Bexley	Harrow.
Kingston-upon-Thames*		

Wales

Conwy	Pembrokeshire	Carmarthenshire*

Scotland

Dundee*	South Lanarkshire*	Fife
Orkney		

Northern Ireland

All five Library and Education Boards are now included in the PLR sample.

* Authorities marked with* were replaced
in 2005/06 by Oxfordshire,
Gloucestershire, Lincolnshire, Wigan,
Redbridge/Havering/Wandsworth,
Swansea, Argyll & Bute, Edinburgh

The Artist's Attic: Story Catcher workshop. The Story Chair; also used by authors and story tellers

Administration

Human Resources and Finance

HR & Finance Manager, Janine Armstrong, takes us through the year.

Human Resources

Our department's aim is to support organisational objectives and empower staff to provide an excellent service.

Research shows that the approaches taken to managing people have the single biggest influence on an organisation's performance and during the year we have again been concentrating on creating an environment in which staff can thrive. We have implemented stress awareness policies and training; conducted health and safety inspections and implemented training; streamlined our staff performance appraisal system to ensure its completion in good time for the annual pay negotiations; introduced a staff suggestions scheme; improved communication and administration of staff pensions and enhanced our accommodation and security.

To help our management team identify the skills they need for their areas of responsibility we have introduced a formal competency framework; and a number of training sessions led by external specialists were held during the year. Much is expected of the management team in terms of administering their own areas of the PLR operation and in taking forward the various development projects currently in hand. In recognition of their achievements in both areas we have introduced a new performance-related pay system.

As an office we have analysed the main risks that could disrupt our administration of PLR, and have developed a staff continuity plan to ensure that we have cover for key functions should staff be prevented from getting to work as a result of any type of major incident.

Objective 5
We met our target of
containing the
Scheme's running
costs within our target
figure of £822,000;
£6.5 million was
distributed to authors
in payments.

Finance

Building on audit advice we have implemented a new system for managing budgets at departmental level with the aim of giving managers more control. This has included separating out IT costs from the wider Corporate Services budget.

A major achievement has been the completion of the PENNY project which has automated all our author payment procedures. This has reduced workloads and has reduced significantly the risk of human error. Staff from both of PLR's main operational teams contributed to this project and its successful implementation means that all PLR systems are now fully automated.

Objective 6
With DCMS, implement
changes to PLR's
legislation raising the
maximum author
payment threshold to
£6,600 and lowering the
minimum threshold to
£1. (Parliamentary
assent received 1 July
2005; new thresholds
come into effect for
February 2007 author
payments.)

Payments to authors were made successfully on 7 February. By meeting our running cost targets we were in a position to free £6.54 million from our funding for distribution to just over 18,500 authors. This included 281 authors who received the maximum payment of £6,000. Over 80% of the PLR Fund was distributed in individual payments of £500 or more. Payments were made on the basis of a rate per loan of 5.57 pence (the highest to date).

Accommodation

For the present, Richard House continues to provide excellent accommodation and our rent and service charges are commensurate with the quality and location of our premises. This year saw improvements to car park lighting and we have installed additional heating to improve the working environment for staff, as well as upgrading the entry system to improve security.

The building was sold in October 2005 and is now managed by a local agent. We will undertake a comprehensive review of our accommodation needs next year. We will then be well placed to take advantage of a break clause in our current lease in 2009 should circumstances require us to consider relocation to alternative premises.

Green Issues

Through our Green Housekeeping Strategy we determine our aims and objectives for conserving energy and resources, purchasing environmentally-friendly products, and recycling and reducing waste. As we move increasingly over to an e-business environment we expect to further reduce our reliance on paper products.

The Team

The Team is led by Janine Armstrong, HR and Finance Manager. She is supported by Lynn Smith, Business Support Officer; Helen Jackson, Business Support Assistant (appointed in November 2005); and Val Greenan, Administration Officer.

Information Technology

PLR's Information Technology Manager, Darren Scrafton, reports.

Information and Communications Technology underpins the whole of the PLR operation. IT and e-Business solutions provided by the IT team are aimed at reducing costs while increasing efficiency, enabling greater benefits for authors and libraries, as well as value-added services for PLR staff.

We support and maintain the growing number of PLR's IT and communications systems, and provide technical expertise for various development projects. Two of these, the development and set-up of an electronic records management system and the automation of the system that records author payments, were completed this year.

ISBN 13

As noted in the Author Services report above, the change in format from 10 to 13 digits has required considerable input in order for us to continue to manage both loans data and authors' registration information accurately. During the year the prototypes prepared by the IT team to deal with all occurrences of ISBNs displayed on screen in PLR systems were approved by the Author Services team and we are currently implementing these across the PLR system. The work is expected to be completed by October 2006.

Electronic Records Management

Objective 7
Design, test and bring into operation new electronic records management system by 31 March 2006. (Achieved.)

We have designed and developed our own in-house electronic records management system for storing and indexing electronic and scanned documents in line with the requirements of the e-government programme. With the initial implementation complete we are now streamlining functionality to ensure that the arrangements sit comfortably with existing workflow systems. The project has also involved extensive work by Sue Ridge and Julia Coxon in devising the filing structure for the new records system.

Our next task will be to finalise integration with word processing and e-mail systems, and with the bespoke PLR applications handling author and book registration, and the collection and processing of loans data. This will enable PLR to handle Freedom of Information (FOI) requests and data collation and dispersal more cost effectively. Resources permitting, we aim to make a start on this work in the coming year.

LEWIS – Loans Enquiry Web Information Service

LEWIS has the potential to provide the library community with access to PLR's unique library loans database. Using a 'data warehousing' approach to provide fast and flexible access to PLR's vast holdings of loans data, the system has been running in-house for over a year now. The next stage is to pilot the prototype by providing access to the database for seven library authorities from June 2006. A dedicated broadband line will provide the libraries with internet access to the system and we look forward to their feedback.

System upgrades

We managed a successful migration to a new database server in August 2005. At the same time we moved to an Open Source version of our Ingres relational database. The Open Source option is more cost effective than previous arrangements, and provides a more flexible environment for in-house staff to develop Ingres software to meet PLR's specific business needs.

Recognition for innovation

"I would like to take this opportunity on behalf of the Advisory Committee to congratulate Darren Scrafton," says Chair, Simon Brett. "His contribution to the development of PLR's IT systems resulted in him being short-listed in the 'Innovator of the Year' category in this year's BT- sponsored Government Computing Awards. Darren came Runner-Up in the contest, a remarkable achievement providing due recognition of his talents and openness to new ideas, and of PLR's commitment to innovation."

IT Team
Darren Scrafton leads the team as IT Manager and is supported by Helen Wadsworth, Technical Specialist.

My Character
Notebook

In each room of the
gallery, look for
characters that interest
you.

What is special about
them? Make notes or
draw them in this special
character notebook

Later, you can use
to create a story
own

Name: _____

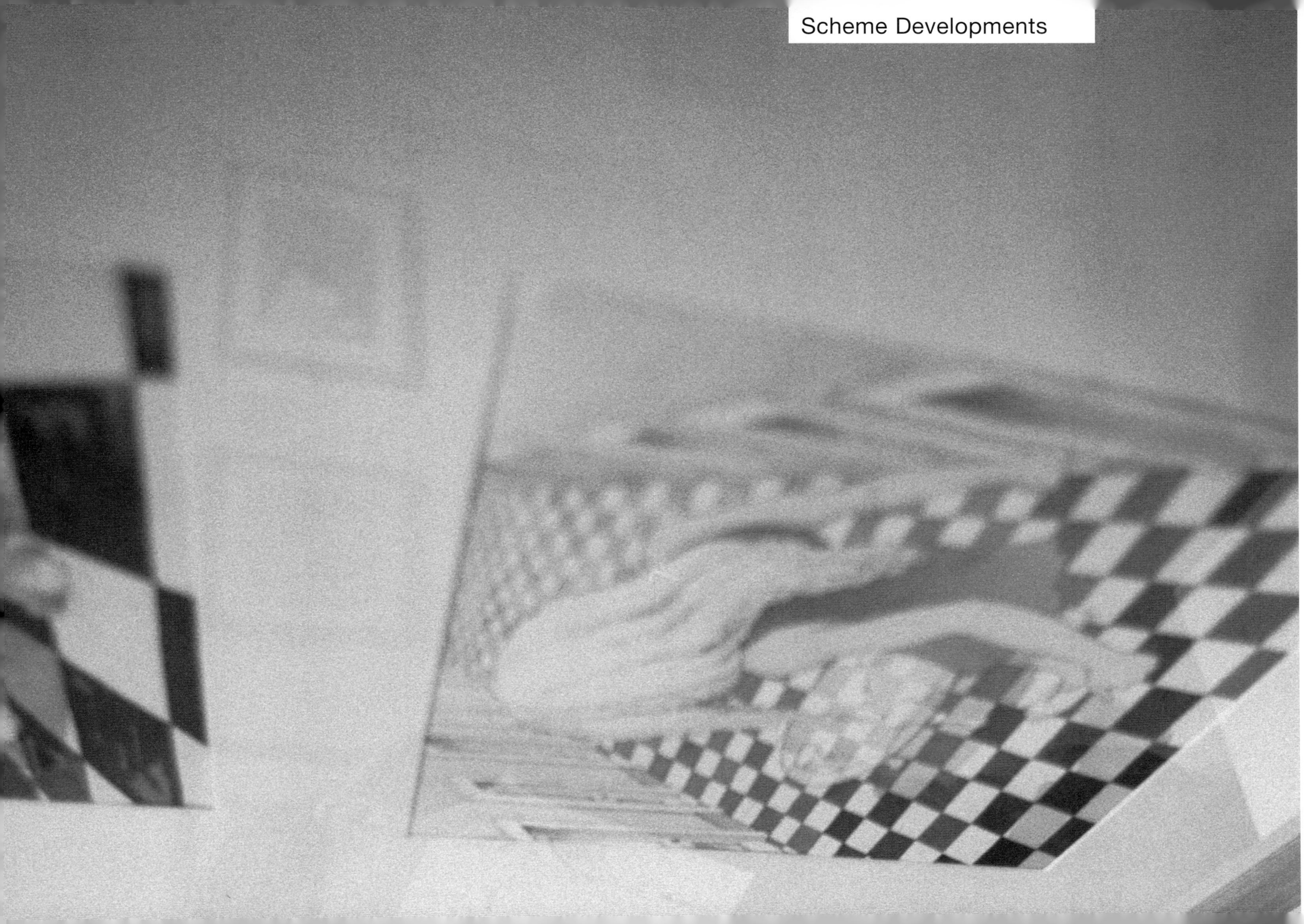

Advisory Committee

Objective 8
Design, test and bring into operation by 31 March 2006 new system for automatic recording of author payments, including electronic accounting procedures for payments 'on hold'. (Achieved.)

Committee chairman, **Simon Brett**, reviews the work of the Committee

There is something very satisfying about being involved in a success, and from my position as Chair of the Advisory Committee I am in no doubt that PLR is a huge success. It always has been. From the moment, over twenty-five years ago, when the aspirations of many tenacious campaigners were realised in the form of legislation, Public Lending Right has become an essential part of the literary landscape. And the most important word in the organisation's name has always been the third. To receive payment from the borrowings of their books is an author's right, and it is wonderful to see how, since the Scheme started, almost all opposition to that concept has evaporated.

On the Advisory Committee I am privileged to work with a very highly qualified group of people, who cover the range of the literary world. There are authors, librarians, agents and representatives of the country's main writers' organisations. Their breadth of knowledge means that, whatever topic arises for discussion, we have experts there to bring us up to date with current thinking and to propose new ideas and solutions.

One of the aims of the Committee is liaison between the PLR office and DCMS, the government department which looks after that area of public life – as well as a great many others. In fact, given the range of responsibilities the DCMS encompasses, I am always impressed by how well briefed the civil servants who attend our meetings are. Then, of course, the Committee includes members of PLR staff. Our Registrar, Jim Parker, is unfailingly patient in explaining the minutiae

of his business to us, and encouragingly open to new ideas. He is always keen to move the PLR system forward, and we strongly support his aims to update and simplify the existing legislation to bring it more in tune with what is actually happening in libraries today.

Jim must know more about PLR systems than anyone else in the world, and it is significant how much of his time he spends advising authorities in countries which have a shorter history of interest in the subject than our own. I am delighted that his exceptional contribution has been recognised by his recent appointment for a fourth term.

So what kind of issues are discussed at an Advisory Committee meeting?

So what kind of issues are discussed at an Advisory Committee meeting? There will be news of ongoing projects – the continuing refinement of the computer system which makes the whole operation run so smoothly, the encouraging increase in authors taking advantage of the on-line registration facility, the constant monitoring of the selection of the libraries which do our sampling. Then there will be discussion of developing initiatives for change within the Scheme – adjustment of payment thresholds, the feasibility of extending PLR to reference books, methods of making more authors aware of their rights, the best ways of using and offering to others the fascinating statistical information about reading habits which the PLR system has produced. And we will have updates on the progress in other countries where, as now fixed in EU legislation, the payment of authors for their library borrowings is becoming a legal right. There are ongoing problems too. In common with most organisations dependent on public funding, PLR is constantly concerned with budgeting and ensuring that the monies granted to us in government spending reviews keep pace with the continuing growth of the Scheme, whether that be in attracting new authors, increasing the size of library samples or many other developing initiatives.

But, whatever the area, I am fortunate in the personnel of the Committee. On any subject, I know I can rely on them for generous contributions of expert opinion and lively informed discussion.

PLR is a big success. I don't think I'd fancy chairing the Advisory Committee of an organisation that wasn't so well run.

Which all goes to make my role as Chair very easy. As I wrote at the beginning of this article, PLR is a big success. I don't think I'd fancy chairing the Advisory Committee of an organisation that wasn't so well run.

The Bookshop: window seat

Communication

How Public Lending Right relates to the outside world is a key strategic strand of its operation. It's vital for the organisation's development that rightsholders, politicians, the business community and the wider public understand PLR's role, contribution to the UK's creative and knowledge economy, and its wider international remit.

The work centres around communication with potential beneficiaries: authors, and all other rightsholders including translators, editors, and illustrators, to ensure they are aware of their right and understand the need to register in order to receive payment.

Underlying this is the need for those who influence and make decisions that have an impact on the creative industries to grasp the value of individuals' contributions. This requires extensive liaison work as PLR works collaboratively with the 'reading industries' – publishers, the library community and the range of agencies that promote authors' rights, reading and writing.

Communication involves several of PLR's key staff, with the support of a consultant. Meetings with our sponsoring department, DCMS, are attended; the Registrar speaks at industry and government conferences and seminars nationally and internationally; there's on-going liaison with authors' organisations and other agencies; articles and papers are written; and a range of public, business and journalists' questions are answered. As with any communication it's a two way process and PLR's staff are endlessly flexible and supportive in answering questions promptly and efficiently.

One of the main strands this year is the continuing work with public library authorities as PLR prepares to share its unique range of data. The LEWIS system is enabling libraries and a wider audience to understand the nation's reading habits and could be used in the future to support decisions on stock selection and management, reading promotions and publishing.

The data produced by LEWIS has provided a vivid and entertaining picture of what we read. The annual media campaign, timed to synchronise with the payment distribution each February, generated massive interest both amongst the national and regional media.

Jacqueline Wilson was the top-lending author for the third successive year and her popularity ensured considerable column inches. However, the information provided by LEWIS indicated a change in our reading habits nationally: we are turning our backs on romantic fiction in favour of crime and thrillers while children's book borrowing continues to thrive.

The headlines generated make interesting reading: *'Love is over for county's readers.'* Dudley Express & Star; *'Libraries say books on buying property in Spain among most popular.' 'Read the book, got the T-shirt, bought the villa.'* Business News (Thames to Gatwick); *'Big rise in number of people using facilities.' 'Revival in lending at libraries?'* Scunthorpe Evening Telegraph; *'Children's writers become library favourites.'* The Guardian; *'Little borrowers give writer big boost.'* The Times.

These headlines help PLR to get noticed and talk to a wide audience: writers and rightsholders, politicians, the library community, the 'reading industries' and the general public. They help to remind everyone just how much we depend on our writers and creators, helping to ensure they are not forgotten as they slave away in their proverbial garrets.

Who holds the right?

Authors are commonly referred to as the beneficiaries of PLR. But the Scheme uses the term 'author' in a generic sense, and there are several groups of contributors to books who have a right to register.

It would be easy to overlook these other rightsholders as their names do not appear in large print on the cover and they don't often make headlines in the way that celebrity authors do. So who are they?

Behind many books destined for public library shelves there is often more than one person whose creative input contributes to the final work. The other contributors referred to include illustrators, photographers, editors and translators – all of whom play a key role in the creative process.

With the global nature of publishing, and the merging of cultures, the written word frequently needs to be translated. If you consider the task of translating poetry or any work of fiction you can appreciate the creativity involved. Not only the required fluency in another language but also the creative ability not to lose any of the original author's intentions in the process. Translators are entitled to a 30% share of the PLR in a book, and more if they can demonstrate additional contributions, such as editorial work. The Advisory Committee has been looking at translators' PLR shares following changes in the allocation granted to them in other areas of authors' rights and expects to make recommendations for consideration by Ministers in the coming year.

Editors also receive recognition, earning 20% of the right. To qualify, an editor must demonstrate that he or she has contributed more than 10% of a book or the equivalent of at least 10 pages of text. Publishing house editors who commission and undertake basic editing work do not qualify. The Scheme also allows editors to top up their share to over 20% if they make further contributions; for example, an editor of a collection or an anthology could claim a larger share if they have contributed stories or chapters themselves. There are also editors who may have contributed considerable research or even a lifetime's work to editing a classic text. In these circumstances the Scheme allows us to increase the percentage and PLR has some registered editors who are earning up to 90%.

And what of ghost writers? They can qualify for payment if they are named on the title page of a book and they can agree their share with the subject of the particular title. They can also qualify if they have a royalty agreement with their publisher. And for those who have no title page credit and received a one-off fee for their work, there is provision for the named 'author' to grant the ghost writer a share by 'amicable agreement'.

Illustrators and photographers are treated in the same way as writers. They receive 100% of the right if the book is all their own work. More commonly they have to agree shares with a writer or other contributors and the PLR office does not get involved in this decision. This is not an exact science but people tend to reach an amicable agreement proportionate to their contribution. Where there are a number of contributors, such as an illustrated children's book that has been translated, the translator would receive a fixed share of 30% and the remaining 70% would then be divided between the writer and illustrator.

Ultimately the aim of the Scheme is to ensure that all creative contributions to any one published book, borrowed from a library, receive due reward for their work.

"When translators go along to talk to the public about their work there's tremendous interest in what we do. Just giving people a very literal version to work on together always provokes lively discussion. Before long people are spending hours arguing over whether the French for 'sandwich' is the same as the English, or how exactly you would transfer incredibly time-specific 2,000-year old jokes by Aristophanes or Catullus into something we would still laugh at today." Jo Balmer, translator.

Matt Parsons, Paper Conservator, dismantles Incredible Journeys. Author/illustrators: Eve Garnett (drawing) *Family from One End Street*; Charles Keeping (painting) *Alfie and the Ferryboat*

International

Objective 9
In partnership with
Spanish author
organisations, plan for
and organise seminar
to be held in Madrid
for existing and
candidate EU Member
States seeking to
establish PLR systems.
(Achieved; seminar
held 23-25 March
2006.)

PLR continues to take the lead in developing Public Lending Right abroad. European Specialist, Janice Forbes, reports on the year's programme of events.

Our work in Europe has two key elements: encouraging European authors to register for PLR here in the UK, and giving help and advice to countries which have just developed, or are looking to develop, their own PLR systems.

We have well-established arrangements to handle the distribution of PLR payments with collecting societies in countries such as Ireland, France, Germany, Estonia and the Netherlands. In 2005-06 we set up an arrangement with Italy and in February Italian writers were paid for the first time via the collecting society SIAE. Making payments through collecting societies is proving an efficient and cost-effective way to distribute payments to European authors.

We are looking forward to working with more collecting societies in European countries both as a means of publicising eligibility for our scheme and ultimately handling payments. We are currently in discussion with collecting societies in Spain (CEDRO) and in Austria (Literar Mechana) with a view to making payments to them for the first time in 2007 to cover loans of books by authors from both countries in public libraries in the UK.

Following discussions with Literar Mechana, which administers the Austrian PLR system, payments were made this year for the first time to UK authors. Incoming payments from foreign PLR systems are handled by our partner organisation, the Authors' Licensing & Collecting Society which already distributes PLR payments from Germany and the Netherlands.

International PLR Network

The Registrar acts as co-ordinator for this Network and we have been supporting development of PLR internationally throughout the year.

There is increased interest in PLR across Europe, both among existing and candidate member states. Recognition of authors' lending rights is a requirement of European Union membership in line with the 1992 Lending Right Directive. Following a successful court case against Belgium for delays in implementing the Directive, the European Commission has been active again during the year in seeking compliance from several other established States such as Ireland, Italy, Portugal and Spain. In these cases, governments had chosen to take advantage of a provision in the Directive allowing Member States to exclude certain categories of library establishment from the requirement to pay PLR. These States had sought to include publicly funded libraries among the institutions to be exempted from PLR. The Commission challenged this interpretation and has been supported in the European courts. PLR legislation is now expected in Ireland later in 2006, and we await news of progress in the other Member States affected by this ruling.

The Commission is also in communication with the governments in several Scandinavian countries which have well-established PLR systems functioning as part of each state's wider support for culture. In these countries books must be written in the country's language to qualify for PLR and the Commission has queried whether this approach is discriminatory.

We have continued to support the development of PLR through advice to individual countries and by involvement with the Network's ongoing series of conferences and seminars. Recent successes include the setting up of systems in newer Member States such as Estonia, Latvia, Lithuania and Slovenia, and PLR legislation is at an advanced stage in the Czech Republic, Slovakia and Hungary. PLR is not, however, restricted to Europe. It remains a truly international right, with systems currently operating in Australia, Canada, Israel and New Zealand. (PLR legislation also exists in Mauritius, but no steps have been taken as yet to set up a payment system.)

International PLR Conference, Berlin, 2005

2005 was the tenth anniversary of the first international PLR conference hosted in the UK. September saw the 6th International PLR conference in Berlin, hosted by the German authors' organisation, VG Wort. In 1995 there were 14 PLR schemes; ten years on there are now 22.

These conferences offer PLR nations the opportunity to discuss issues and developments across the PLR arena and to share experiences. The Berlin conference saw presentations of the new UK and Estonian on-line registration systems, and an update from the European Commission on implementation of the Lending Right Directive. There was also a debate on the potential for discrimination in an EU context of the language eligibility criteria operated by some of the Scandinavian PLR systems.

PLR Seminar, Madrid, 2006

This was the third seminar organised to support the development of PLR systems in EU member states. Hosted by the Spanish authors organisation, ACE, 20 countries sent representatives. Aimed at countries yet to establish systems, delegates were drawn from a range of sectors: government departments, library and author organisations. The diversity of attendees allowed for a broad

n Eyes by David Almond

ヘヴン・アイズ

定価 本体1500円 (税込)

C0097 ¥1500E

ISBN4-309-20397-20

1920097015000

discussion of the issues faced in these countries and provided an opportunity for candidate countries, such as Romania and Croatia, to benefit from best practice elsewhere. The Registrar gave a presentation summarising the current European situation and chaired a number of the discussion sessions.

International Website

The Network website (www.plrinternational.com) is administered from the UK PLR office. It has established itself as a key reference site for information on international PLR developments. It is being redesigned, and will include information on the new PLR systems, news, conference reports and links to national PLR websites.

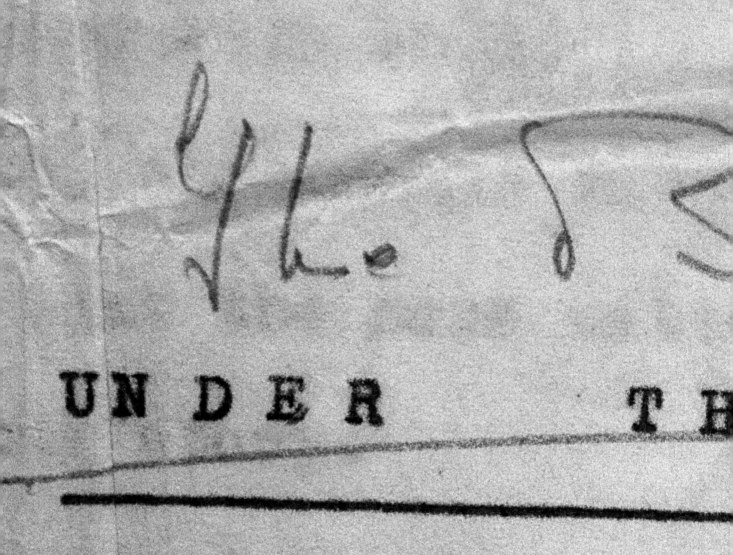

UNDER ... TH

Public Lending Right and the Authors' Licensing & Collecting Society (ALCS) share a common aim: that of supporting and advocating the rights of creators of written works whether published or broadcast. These creators are at the very core of a burgeoning creative economy. Former Chief Executive of ALCS **Jane Carr** takes a look at the broader context in which they operate and the need for proper recognition to ensure both their contributions and the creative economy can be sustained.

Authors and the Creative Economy

As the source of the creative economy, the creator deserves and needs recognition, protection and reward.

"Creativity, properly employed, carefully evaluated, skillfully managed and soundly implemented, is a key to future business success – and to national prosperity."
The Cox Review of Creativity in Business: Building on the UK's strengths, September 2005

The creative economy is increasingly seen as of major importance to the future prosperity of the UK, and of Europe. It is creation and innovation that can give the UK and Europe a competitive edge in an increasingly global, digital environment – and the source of the creative economy is ultimately the individual creator.

In October 2005 the UK hosted the Creative Economy Conference as part of the EU Presidency programme. Speaking at the Conference, Lord Sainsbury, Minister for Science & Technology, summarised the situation: "Offering consumers compelling new content in innovative ways, simple for the consumer to use and at a fair price must be the way forward for all the creative industries."

Both Tessa Jowell, Secretary of State for Culture, Media and Sport, and Lord Sainsbury have stressed the vital role that creativity and innovation will make in the virtual, digital marketplace; a marketplace where the currency of trade is ideas and information as much as goods and services. Both of them have also recognised the vital role of creators in the digital supply chain, and their need for recognition and reward.
At the Creative Economy Conference, Tessa Jowell asserted that 'fair

The creative economy is thus central both to our society's economic and cultural well-being.

rewards for creativity' are essential to a flourishing creative economy. In his speech to the Social Market Foundation on 'Innovating for Success' (February 2006), Lord Sainsbury noted that 'it is crucial that we educate young people about intellectual property so they respect the time, energy and resources that have gone into their latest purchase'.

That wider consumer recognition of the central position of the creator in the emerging digital economy is vital if continuity of creativity and innovation are to be sustained. Whether a writer, illustrator, photographer, translator or editor; a composer or a cartoonist, an inventor of games or a stand-up comic, much of the work of creation is undertaken by individuals or small collaborative groups. In many cases it is those individuals or small groups who invest in their own talent, not large corporations, and this aspect of creativity needs to be better understood by the general public.

Creators feel vulnerable in many ways. The most immediate vulnerability is personal; the offering of a creative work to a critical public. The longer-term vulnerability is economic. The reasons behind this, most of which are inevitable in the creative process, must be recognised if creativity and innovation are to be sustained.

The first economic risk that the creator has to consider is how to fund the creative process. Book advances rarely cover the time taken to create them, except in the case of a few well-established, best-selling writers; a commissioned work of journalism or music may be purchased outright at an agreed price, but full payment will only be on delivery of the finished work and may bear no relation to the time taken to create it.

At the stage of commissioning, the creator is almost always the weaker party. Contractual negotiations are an imperative to form a partnership for the dissemination of a work, whether with a publisher, broadcaster, record company or theatre manager.

As the source of the creative economy, the creator deserves and needs recognition, protection and reward. Recognition for the creator is, to some extent, provided by the assertion of moral rights (of paternity and freedom from derogatory use). In parts of the European Community the author's moral rights are inalienable and, in a digital world, this may be a step that the UK should seriously consider.

To some extent protection is also provided through copyright and the partnerships between creators and producers. These partnerships are essential to the successful development of the creative economy and to continuity in the creative process. The reward (whether financial or other) should come as a recognition both of the investment the creator makes and of the value of the work itself, over time. However this is not always the case.

Important as the economic arguments are to the future of the creative economy, the cultural and social contribution of creators is at least of equal significance in the longer term. Creators provide the diversity of information, education, entertainment and enrichment that are essential to the development of society and to consumers of all ages. The significance of the creator to successful societies is internationally recognised and referenced in Points 16 and 17 of the Preamble to the UNESCO Convention on the Protection and Promotion of the Diversity of Cultural Expression (2005).

The Convention recognizes the creator's essential role in society. It also recognises the need to protect creators and their works so that they can continue to produce original ideas, whether of fact or imagination, and in doing so encourage others to create and innovate themselves:

The Convention notes the value of: 'Emphasizing the vital role of cultural interaction and creativity, which nurture and renew cultural expressions and enhance the role played by those involved in the development of culture for the progress of society at large. Recognizing the importance of intellectual property rights in sustaining those involved in cultural creativity.'

The creative economy is thus central both to our society's economic and cultural well-being. Public Lending Right is one of the hard won but essential means by which we can ensure that creativity is sustainable for the future.

"Intellectual property is the oil of the 21st Century."
Mark Getty, The Economist, 2000.

PLR Central Fund Account
for the year ended
31 March 2006

PUBLIC LENDING RIGHT
CENTRAL FUND ACCOUNT 2005 - 2006

Management Commentary

These are the accounts for the twenty third year of the Public Lending Right (PLR) Central Fund and cover the annual payments due to authors at 31 March 2006.

History and Statutory Background

The Public Lending Right Act 1979 established a right for authors to receive remuneration from public funds in respect of their books lent out from public libraries. The calculation of library loans is estimated from a sample of public libraries where issues are recorded electronically and processed by local authority computers before transmission to the Registrar's computer at Stockton-on-Tees: for the twenty third year's calculations the number of library authorities in the sample was 39.

The details of eligible books, eligible authors, and payment calculations are set out in The Public Lending Right Scheme 1982, as amended in 1983, 1984, 1988, 1989 and 1990. The consolidated text appears in Statutory Instrument 1990 No 2360. Further amendments were made in Statutory Instruments 1991 No 2618, 1993 No 799, 1996 No 3237, 1997 No 1576, 1998 No 1218, 1999 Nos 420, 905, 3304, 2000 Nos 933, 3319, 2001 No 3984, 2002 No 3123, 2003 No 839, 2003 No 3045, 2004 No 1258, 2004 No 3128, 2005 No 1519, 2005 No 3351.

The Public Lending Right Advisory Committee advises the Secretary of State for Culture, Media and Sport and the Registrar on the operation of the Scheme but has no formal responsibility for the management of PLR. Appointments to the Committee are made by the Secretary of State. Details of the Committee's membership at 31 March 2006 are provided in Annex A.

Review of Activities

The twenty third year's operations are described in the PLR Annual Report which includes the statutory report on the operation of the Scheme laid before Parliament by the Secretary of State for Culture, Media and Sport.

Payments to Authors

PLR's core funding from DCMS was increased to £7.419 million (£7.381 million in 2004-2005). On the basis of the increased funding, it proved possible to increase the level of the rate per loan for the February 2006 payments to authors to 5.57 pence, the highest figure to date (5.26 pence in 2004-2005). A total sum of £6,597,000 was made available from the Central Fund for paying out to 18,584 authors. 82% of the Fund was distributed in payments of £500 or more.

18,584 authors and assignees (18,666 in 2004-2005) qualified for payments. The numbers of authors in the various payment categories were as follows:-

Authors Earning:	Twenty Third Year	Twenty Second Year
£6,000.00	281	285
£5,000.00 - £5,999.99	68	70
£2,500.00 £4,999.99	390	376
£1,000.00 £2,499.99	782	783
£500.00 £999.99	959	911
£100.00 £499.99	3,725	3,826
£50.00 - £99.99	2,403	2,518
£5.00 - £49.99	9,976	9,897
	18,584	18,666
Expenditure	6,543,164	6,536,539

Expenditure includes £34,574 still to be paid at the year end. These authors' addresses are unknown to PLR, or their assignees have not made probate claims. A further £12,243 is a separate provision which is used to supplement the central fund. There were 15,871 (15,011 in 2004-2005) authors whose books earned no payment.

An analysis of the distribution of money for the twenty third year to authors by payment category shows:

	£	%
£6,000.00	1,691,026	25.84
£5,000.00 - £5,999.99	369,943	5.65
£2,500.00 - £4,999.99	1,375,132	21.02
£1,000.00 - £2,499.99	1,228,987	18.78
£500.00 - £999.99	676,348	10.34
£100.00 - £499.99	840,127	12.84
£50.00 - £99.99	171,187	2.62
£5.00 - £49.99	190,414	2.91
		100.00

Risks and Uncertainties

We feel that our particular strengths lie in certain key areas of the Scheme's administration: openness to modernisation and new ideas, emphasis on maintaining cost-effective systems, responsiveness to authors' needs and concerns. We feel that the success of our staff in each of these areas is a source of great strength for the PLR organisation. The high regard in which the PLR team is held by authors once again came through in the 99% satisfaction rating received in feedback from authors registering with PLR.

Risk management is now central to our planning systems and PLR's Risk Register is kept under continuous review by the Registrar, the Audit Committee and PLR's management team. The most significant risk to our management of the Scheme that we face in the coming year is the impact of the book trade's conversion to 13-digit ISBNs. This will affect all our book registration, loans data collection and processing, and payment operations. It requires significant changes to PLR IT programs and applications. This work is being managed as a formal project under the Prince2 project guidelines and we are confident of its success.

Other risks relate to the relative smallness of the PLR operation and our reliance on external suppliers of services. These include the risks to the effective management of the Scheme posed by trying to cope with central government and other initiatives ('initiative overload'); and the risk of failing to meet business targets as a result of inadequate planning. We aim to manage these risks by use of best-practice project management procedures which will give advance warning of overload problems; by a constant emphasis on efficiency and use of new technologies to enable us to achieve more with existing resources; and by promoting and maintaining good relations with partner bodies on whom we rely for services. PLR is acutely aware of the consequences of not managing these risks effectively and the adverse effect it could have on our authors.

Development and Performance of the Business

Our priority over the last year has been to administer the PLR Scheme efficiently, cost-effectively and fairly, with the emphasis on providing authors with the best service possible. Of our key performance indicators the most important related to running costs and required us to hold these at a level agreed with DCMS in our Funding Agreement and Efficiency Delivery Plan. This we achieved, in spite of the continued growth of the Scheme (eg 1,400 new authors registered, the highest annual increase in ten years) enabling us to distribute £6.54 million in payments to authors in February. We also were able to continue with our modernisation plans: we completed work on the automation of author payment records, and implemented phase one of our electronic records management system. Both systems were designed by our own IT team to take account of PLR's specific needs. There continues to be great demand from authors and libraries for more fully-developed access to our unique database.

PLR's performance is measured by regular assessment of our progress in achieving the agreed Funding Agreement targets in the table below, performance against PLR's Delivery Plans and performance against the efficiency targets.

FUNDING AGREEMENT TARGETS 05-08	2005-06	STATUS	2006-07 PLANS
1. Efficiency Savings Meet efficiency targets (based on 04/05 operating cost, adjusted for inflation)	2.5%	✓	5%
2. Author Satisfaction Maintain high stakeholder satisfaction rate (based on survey of registered authors)	95%	✓	95%
3. Library Satisfaction Maintain high stakeholder satisfaction rate (based on survey of sample libraries)	95%	✓	95%
4. Speed and Accuracy Achieve high stakeholder satisfaction rates (based on author survey)	95%	✓	95%
5. Increase % of registration transactions undertaken via on-line registration service to meet the following targets (taking the 2004-05 figure of 40% as the baseline)	45%	✓	50%

Delivery Plan

PLR's Delivery Plan provides details of the strategic objectives agreed with DCMS. Strategic objectives achieved in 2005-2006 include:

1)   Administer PLR to meet the legal requirements of the PLR Act and Scheme

        Outcomes achieved were: a)   complete by 31.7.05 registration of all application forms received before 30.6.05

                                               b)   introduce required number of new library authorities to sample and complete sample data collection by 31.10.05

2)   Expand the Scheme to bring in more authors and extend the library sample while meeting efficiency targets

        Outcomes Achieved were: a)   continue to absorb growing author and book registrations (average 1,200 new authors per year)

                                               b)   continue to increase size of library sample to improve representativeness of loans data collected over the 3 year Funding Agreement period (increase from 38 to 39 sample authorities from July 2005)

Sustainable Development

PLR's Green Strategy promotes energy saving throughout the office in order to improve energy efficiency. This is achieved by a range of measures, including energy efficient lighting and double-glazing; office equipment with energy saving features; electrical equipment switched off at night; staff awareness training. Our IS Strategy requires all IT and telecommunications equipment to be purchased in accordance with the *Restriction of the use of Certain Hazardous Substances in Electrical & Electronic Equipment Regulations 2005*. Our investment in IT has improved our overall performance, reduced our environmental impact (eg our move away from paper-based communications with the introduction of the electronic records management system) and demonstrates to our stakeholders that we are managing our environmental risks responsibly as well as making cost savings.

Local and Regional

PLR maintains close links with local authority library services. Partnerships with public libraries are essential for the efficient and timely collection of the loans data required for calculating the payments made to authors under the PLR Scheme; and increasingly we are supporting the Department's Framework for the Future agenda for libraries through the development of our new loans data service (LEWIS) which will ultimately enable libraries to access PLR's unique database of information on book borrowing trends. In this we are working closely with partners such as The Reading Agency and the Museums, Libraries and Archives Council who have strong local and regional links.

Fixed Assets

No land or buildings are owned. No funds are accumulated for the replacement of other assets. Future replacement will need to be financed from funds voted in the year of acquisition.

Movements on fixed assets are set out in note 6 to the financial statements.

Payment of Creditors

The Registrar adheres to the Government-wide standard for payment of bills by aiming to settle all bills within thirty days. In 2005-2006, 99% of creditor invoices were paid within 30 days of being received (2004-2005, 99%). Every effort is also made by PLR to effect payments to authors on the annual date fixed by the Registrar. However, as a result of failure by authors to notify PLR of changes in address or bank details, and of other circumstances outside the control of the Registrar, it may not always be possible to make payment. In such cases, the Registrar is required to hold payments as debts due to the authors concerned for up to six years during which period all reasonable efforts are made by PLR to effect payment.

Superannuation

The PCSPS is a "pay-as-you-go" statutory unfunded pension scheme. In accordance with Section 40 of the Social Security Pensions Act 1975 such schemes are exempted from the need to set up funds. The liability to pay pensions is underwritten by an understanding that in accordance with existing legislation, in particular the Superannuation Act 1972, the Government is obliged to provide benefits to members of such schemes in accordance with their respective rules.

Results and Appropriations

The Fund is distributed after deduction of the Registrar's remuneration, administrative costs, and payments to local authorities. The surplus for the year was £74,771 (2005, £18,324). As a result, the Central Fund ended the year with a surplus carried forward of £97,804.

Future developments

In terms of modernisation the main thrust of our project work continues to be in the area of e-business. We look forward to completing the final phases of our on-line registration, electronic records management and LEWIS systems over the next two years. At the same time we shall be taking forward with the Advisory Committee a review of the Scheme's operation to help us identify scope for efficiencies in its operation.

Staffing Matters

The Registrar of Public Lending Right is committed to promoting effective consultation and communications with his staff. PLR's Corporate and Author Services Teams have regular staff meetings at which matters relating to PLR's activities are discussed. Additionally, staff are briefed on matters discussed at senior management and planning meetings. PLR recognises the Public and Commercial Services Union for the purpose of collective bargaining.

The Registrar of Public Lending Right makes every effort to employ disabled people in suitable employment and gives full and fair consideration to applications for employment of disabled people.

Organisation

The PLR Act (1979) gives the Registrar sole corporate responsibility for the PLR Scheme. The PLR Advisory Committee provides advice to the Registrar and DCMS Ministers on aspects of the Scheme's operation. For the last two years, the day-to-day management of the Scheme has been undertaken by Author and Corporate Services teams reporting through Managers to the Assistant Registrar. This devolution of responsibility enables the Registrar to concentrate on strategic and developmental issues.

The Euro

The activities of Public Lending Right are mainly within the United Kingdom. Exposure to transactions denominated in the Euro occurs in respect of authors resident overseas. These are treated no differently from transactions in any foreign currency. Public Lending Right's systems are accordingly already Euro-enabled.

Auditors

The audit of the Public Lending Right Central Fund accounts is carried out by the Comptroller and Auditor General under section 2(6) of the Public Lending Right Act 1979.

As far as the Registrar is aware, there is no relevant audit information of which PLR's auditors are unaware.

The Registrar has taken all the steps that he ought to have taken to make himself aware of any relevant audit information and to establish that PLR's auditors are aware of that information.

J G PARKER
Registrar

28 June 2006

Annex A

PLR Advisory Committee

The members of the Advisory Committee during the year were:

Mr Simon Brett (Chairman)

Dr James Parker, OBE (Registrar of PLR)

Mr Tony Bradman

Ms Gill Coleridge *(Reappointed 29 October 2005)*

Mr Rob Froud

Dr Maggie Gee

Ms Miranda McKearney, OBE

Dr Barry Turner

Ms Jane Carr (Authors' Licensing & Collecting Society), Dr Bob McKee (Chartered Institute of Library and Information Professionals), Mr Mark Le Fanu OBE (Society of Authors) and Mr Bernie Corbett (Writers' Guild of Great Britain) also attended Committee meetings as assessors.

Other than the Registrar, none of the Advisory Committee members received any remuneration from PLR.

PLR Audit Committee

The members of the Audit Committee during the year were:

Mr Mike Dewsnap (Chairman)

Mr Mike Duffy *(Resigned 17 November 2005)*

Ms Pat Hunt *(Appointed 18 November 2005)*

Dr James Parker, OBE

Remuneration Report

Registrar's Salary and Superannuation

As specified in the Act, the Registrar's own remuneration and superannuation costs are charged directly against the £7,471,000 grant due to be made available. As they are not made from the Central Fund, they do not appear in these accounts. A reconciliation to the grant received is shown at note 2. In 2005-2006 the total deduction was £71,620 (2004-2005 £69,538).

The Registrar is appointed by the Secretary of State for Culture, Media and Sport. He is employed on the basis of five-year appointment (renewable) and the terms of his appointment are as set out in the schedule to the PLR Act (1979).

A remuneration committee meets annually to assess the Registrar's performance and, if appropriate, to recommend to Ministers a pay award on the basis of criteria set out in terms of reference provided by DCMS. The whole of any annual pay award to the Registrar is performance-based. Pay awards to the Registrar are dependent on the approval of DCMS Ministers. The committee acts in consultation with DCMS whose advice on wider government pay policy informs the committee's annual recommendations.

The Registrar provides the committee with an annual report setting out in detail his success in meeting KPIs agreed with DCMS. The committee may call for further information if required.

Members of the Committee during the year were:

Mr Simon Brett (Chairman)
Ms Gill Coleridge
Mr Mark Le Fanu, OBE

The Registrar's total remuneration is determined by DCMS. It consisted of a basic salary of £58,157 plus a non-consolidated bonus of £6,776 (2004-2005 total emoluments were made up of £56,464 basic salary plus a non-consolidated bonus of £6,578).

	Age	Salary (including Performance Pay)	Real increase in Pension at age 60	Total accrued pension at age 60 at 31.3.06
Dr James Parker	53	64,933	852 (834 in 2004-05)	10,657 (9,491 in 2004-05)

The Registrar receives no benefits in kind.

The Registrar's appointment has been renewed for a period of five years from 1 August 2006.

RESPONSIBILITIES OF THE REGISTRAR AND DCMS ACCOUNTING OFFICER

Under section 2(6) of the Public Lending Right Act 1979, the Registrar is required to prepare a statement of accounts for the Public Lending Right Central Fund for each financial year in the form and on the basis determined by the Secretary of State for Culture, Media and Sport, with the consent of the Treasury. The accounts are prepared on an accruals basis and must show a true and fair view of the Central Fund's state of affairs at the year end and of its income and expenditure and cash flows for the financial year.

In preparing the accounts the Registrar is required to:

■ observe the accounts direction issued[1] by the Secretary of State, including the relevant accounting and disclosure requirements, and apply suitable accounting policies on a consistent basis;

■ make judgements and estimates on a reasonable basis;

■ state whether applicable accounting standards have been followed, and disclose and explain any material departures in the financial statements; and

■ prepare the financial statements on the going concern basis, unless it is inappropriate to presume that the Central Fund will continue in operation.

The Accounting Officer of the Department for Culture, Media and Sport is the Accounting Officer for payments to the Registrar.

Under Section 2(1) of the Public Lending Right Act 1979, the Central Fund is placed under the management and control of the Registrar who is also responsible for the keeping of proper records. The Accounting Officer of the Department for Culture, Media and Sport has designated the Registrar as the Accounting Officer for the use of, and expenditure from, the Central Fund. As Accounting Officer he has overall responsibility for the propriety and regularity of the Public Lending Right Central Fund finances for which he is answerable to Parliament and for the keeping of proper records. His responsibilities as Accounting Officer are set out in the Accounting Officer's Memorandum issued by the Treasury and published in Government Accounting.

[1] A copy of the accounts direction can be obtained from the following address: Public Lending Right, Richard House, Sorbonne Close, Stockton-on-Tees, TS17 6DA.

J G Parker
Registrar

28 June 2006

STATEMENT OF INTERNAL CONTROL

As Accounting Officer, I have responsibility for maintaining a sound system of internal control that supports the achievement of PLR policies, aims and objectives, whilst safeguarding the public funds and assets for which I am personally responsible, in accordance with the responsibilities assigned to me in Government Accounting and ensuring compliance with the requirements of PLR's Management Statement and Financial Memorandum.

The system of internal control is designed to manage rather than eliminate the risk of failure to achieve policies, aims and objectives; it can therefore only provide reasonable and not absolute assurance of effectiveness.

The system of internal control takes account of Treasury guidance and is based on an ongoing process designed to identify the principal risks to the achievement of PLR policies, aims and objectives, to evaluate the nature and extent of those risks and to manage them efficiently, effectively and economically.

Following some further risk management training last year from our internal auditors our system has been firmly embedded in our operating systems throughout the year. As part of our approach we now identify our objectives and risks and have determined a control strategy for each of the significant risks. A risk management policy document has been sent to all staff setting out PLR's risk strategy.

The Registrar's management team has been reviewing risk management and internal control on a regular basis during the year and there has been a full risk and control assessment before reporting on the year ending 31 March 2006.

PLR employs internal auditors who operate to standards defined in the Government Internal Audit Standards. They submit regular reports which include an independent opinion on the adequacy and effectiveness of PLR's system of internal control together with the recommendations for improvement.

The Audit Committee receives periodic reports from PLR's internal auditors concerning internal control. The internal auditors work closely with PLR's managers on the steps needed to manage risks in their areas of responsibility.

My review of the effectiveness of the system of internal control is informed by the work of the internal auditors and PLR's executive managers who have responsibility for the development and maintenance of the internal control framework, and comments made by the external auditors in their management letter and other reports. I am also guided in this regard by the Audit Committee which advises me on the effectiveness of PLR's internal control systems. In addition to overall annual audit assurance and regular block reports on which to base its advice, the Committee receives copies of PLR's Corporate Plan and other strategy documents; details of key risks and lists of other evidence used by the Registrar to assess the robustness of PLR control systems; and regular progress reports on PLR's implementation of outstanding audit recommendations.

In light of the evidence available to me, I believe that PLR has had all the necessary risk management and review processes in place throughout 2005-2006.

J G Parker
Registrar

28 June 2006

PUBLIC LENDING RIGHT CENTRAL FUND

The Certificate and Report of the Comptroller and Auditor General to the Houses of Parliament

I certify that I have audited the financial statements of Public Lending Right for the year ended 31 March 2006 under the Public Lending Right Act 1979. These comprise the Income and Expenditure Account, the Balance Sheet, the Cashflow Statement and Statement of Recognised Gains and Losses and the related notes. These financial statements have been prepared under the accounting policies set out within them.

Respective responsibilities of the Registrar, the Accounting Officer of the Department for Culture, Media and Sport, and the Auditor

As described on page 82 the Accounting Officer of the Department for Culture, Media and Sport has responsibility for payments into the Public Lending Right Central Fund and to the Registrar. The Registrar, as Accounting Officer for the use of and expenditure from the Public Lending Right Central Fund, is responsible for preparing the Annual Report, the Remuneration Report and the financial statements in accordance with the Public Lending Right Act 1979 and directions made thereunder by the Secretary of State for Culture, Media and Sport and for ensuring the regularity of financial transactions.

My responsibility is to audit the financial statements in accordance with relevant legal and regulatory requirements, and with International Standards on Auditing (UK and Ireland).

I report to you my opinion as to whether the financial statements give a true and fair view and whether the financial statements and the part of the Remuneration Report to be audited have been properly prepared in accordance with the Public Lending Right Act 1979 and directions made thereunder by the Secretary of State for Culture, Media and Sport. I also report whether in all material respects the expenditure and income have been applied to the purposes intended by Parliament and the financial transactions conform to the authorities which govern them. I also report to you if, in my opinion, the Annual Report is not consistent with the financial statements, if Public Lending Right has not kept proper accounting records, if I have not received all the information and explanations I require for my audit, or if information specified by relevant authorities regarding remuneration and other transactions is not disclosed.

I review whether the statement on page 83 reflects Public Lending Right's compliance with HM Treasury's guidance on the Statement on Internal Control, and I report if it does not. I am not required to consider whether the Accounting Officer's statements on internal control cover all risks and controls, or form an opinion on the effectiveness of Public Lending Right's corporate governance procedures or its risk and control procedures.

I read the other information contained in the Annual Report and consider whether it is consistent with the audited financial statements. This other information comprises only the Registrar's Annual Review, the Management Commentary and the unaudited part of the Remuneration Report. I consider the implications for my report if I become aware of any apparent misstatements or material inconsistencies with the financial statements. My responsibilities do not extend to any other information.

Basis of audit opinion

I conducted my audit in accordance with International Standards on Auditing (UK and Ireland) issued by the Auditing Practices Board. My audit includes examination, on a test basis, of evidence relevant to the amounts, disclosures and regularity of financial transactions included in the financial statements and the part of the Remuneration Report to be audited. It also includes an assessment of the significant estimates and judgments made by the Registrar in the preparation of the financial statements, and of whether the accounting policies are most appropriate to the Central Fund's circumstances, consistently applied and adequately disclosed.

I planned and performed my audit so as to obtain all the information and explanations which I considered necessary in order to provide me with sufficient evidence to give reasonable assurance that the financial statements and the part of the Remuneration Report to be audited are free from material misstatement, whether caused by fraud or error and that in all material respects the expenditure and income have been applied to the purposes intended by Parliament and the financial transactions conform to the authorities which govern them. In forming my opinion I also evaluated the overall adequacy of the presentation of information in the financial statements and the part of the Remuneration Report to be audited.

Opinion

In my opinion:

- the financial statements give a true and fair view, in accordance with the Public Lending Right Act 1979 and directions made thereunder by the Secretary of State for Culture, Media and Sport of the state of the Public Lending Right Central Fund affairs as at 31 March 2006 and of its surplus for the year then ended;
- the financial statements and the part of the Remuneration Report to be audited have been properly prepared in accordance with the Public Lending Right Act 1979 and directions made thereunder by the Secretary of State for Culture, Media and Sport; and
- in all material respects the expenditure and income have been applied to the purposes intended by Parliament and the financial transactions conform to the authorities which govern them.

I have no observations to make on these financial statements.

John Bourn
Comptroller and Auditor General
6 July 2006

National Audit Office
157-197 Buckingham Palace Road
Victoria
London SW1W 9SP

PUBLIC LENDING RIGHT CENTRAL FUND

INCOME AND EXPENDITURE ACCOUNT
FOR THE YEAR ENDED 31 MARCH 2006

INCOME	Notes	£	2005-06 £	2004-05 £
HM Government Grant	2	7,399,380		7,402,962
Less: Transferred to Government grant reserve	3	(22,229)		(11,361)
Other Operating Income	4	16,156		18,675
Total income available to PLR Central Fund			7,393,307	7,410,276
EXPENDITURE				
Staff Costs	5	(417,301)		(460,478)
Depreciation	6	(14,210)		(18,531)
Other Operating Charges	7	(357,384)		(393,471)
Public Lending Right to Authors		(6,543,164)		(6,536,539)
			7,332,059	7,409,019
Operating Surplus	8		61,248	1,257
Income from other activities - interest receivable		13,383		15,199
- pension account	9	872		847
			14,255	16,046
Surplus on ordinary activities before taxation			75,503	17,303
Corporation Tax	21		(732)	1,021
Notional Return on Capital	17		2,497	772
Surplus after Notional Income			77,268	19,096
Reversal of Notional Income			(2,497)	(772)
Surplus for the Financial Year			74,771	18,324
Retained Surplus brought forward			23,033	4,709
Retained Surplus carried forward			97,804	23,033

The income and expenditure relate to continuing activities.
The Fund has no recognised gains and losses other than those above and consequently no separate statement of total recognised gains and losses has been presented.
The notes on pages 88 to 97 form part of these accounts.

PUBLIC LENDING RIGHT CENTRAL FUND

BALANCE SHEET AS AT 31 MARCH 2006

	Notes		2005-06	2004-05
		£	£	£
FIXED ASSETS				
Tangible Assets	6		19,090	11,071
CURRENT ASSETS				
Debtors	10	27,462		24,958
Cash at Bank and In Hand		198,320		147,808
		225,782		172,766
CREDITORS				
Amounts falling due within one year	11	(115,735)		(140,125)
Net Current Assets			110,047	32,641
Total Assets Less Current Liabilities			129,137	43,712
FINANCED BY:				
CAPITAL AND RESERVES				
Government Grant Reserve	3		19,090	11,071
Public Lending Right Reserve	12		12,243	9,608
Income and Expenditure Account			97,804	23,033
			129,137	43,712

The notes on pages 88 to 97 form part of these accounts.

J G Parker
Registrar

28 June 2006

PUBLIC LENDING RIGHT CENTRAL FUND

cash flow statement
for the year ended 31 march 2006

	Notes	2005-06 £	2004-05 £
Net Cash Inflow from Operating Activities	13	37,391	13,058
NET CASH INFLOW FROM Returns on Investment and Servicing of Finance			
Interest Received	21	13,370	15,114
Taxation			
Corporation Tax Paid		(1,121)	442
NET CASH OUTFLOW FROM Capital Expenditure and Financial Investment			
Purchase of Fixed Assets	6	(22,229)	(11,361)
NET CASH INFLOW FROM Pensions Account	9	872	847
NET CASH INFLOW FROM Financing			
Government Grant Applied to Capital	3	22,229	11,361
Increase in Cash	14	50,512	29,461

The notes on pages 88 to 97 form part of these accounts.

NOTES TO THE ACCOUNTS AT 31 MARCH 2006

NOTE 1   ACCOUNTING POLICIES

ACCOUNTING CONVENTION

These accounts are prepared under the historical cost convention, as modified by the revaluation of certain fixed assets. Without limiting the information given, the accounts meet the accounting and disclosure requirements of the Companies Act and Accounting Standards issued or adopted by the Accounting Standards Board so far as those requirements are appropriate.

ASSETS AND DEPRECIATION

Fixed assets are accounted for using modified historic cost accounting. However, adjustments to the net book value are only made where material and no such adjustments were made in 2005-2006.

Depreciation is provided on all tangible fixed assets at rates calculated to write off the cost or valuation, less the estimated residual value of each asset, evenly over its expected useful life. Items under £1,000 are written off in the year of purchase. Items over £1,000 are depreciated evenly over 3 years for computer equipment and 5 years for fixtures and fittings.

VALUE ADDED TAX

PLR is outside the scope of VAT.

HM GOVERNMENT GRANT

The capital element of the Grant from the Department for Culture, Media and Sport is credited to a Government Grant Reserve and released to revenue over the expected useful life of the relevant assets. The revenue element of the Grant is credited to income in the year to which it relates.

LEASES

Costs relating to operating leases are charged to the income and expenditure account over the life of the lease.

PENSIONS

Past and present employees are covered by the provisions of the Principal Civil Service Pension Schemes (PCSPS). The defined benefit elements of the schemes are unfunded and are non-contributory except in respect of dependant's benefits. The Central Fund recognises the expected costs of these elements on a systematic and rational basis over the period during which it benefits from the employees' services by payment to the PCSPS of amounts calculated on an accruing basis. Liability for payment of future benefits is a charge on the PCSPS.

NOTIONAL COSTS

In accordance with Treasury guidance, notional costs of capital (calculated at 3.5% of the average capital employed) are charged in the Income and Expenditure Account in arriving at the "Surplus after Notional Costs". These are reversed so that no provision is included in the balance sheet.

NOTE 2   HM GOVERNMENT GRANT

	2005-06 £	2004-05 £
Grant for PLR (DCMS RfR1)	7,471,000	7,472,500
LESS Registrar's Costs	(71,620)	(69,538)
Grant to Central Fund	7,399,380	7,402,962

For 2005-2006 the government grant announced in the 2002 Spending Review was £7,419,000. A further £52,000 has been provided by DCMS to meet PLR's increased superannuation charges following the move of staff to the PCSPS.

The Registrar's Costs comprise the salary and National Insurance payments of the present Registrar. The Registrar's pension scheme is unfunded.

The difference between the Registrar's salary shown in the remuneration report of £64,933 and the Registrar's Costs shown above of £71,620 is employer's National Insurance contributions of £6,687.

NOTE 3   GOVERNMENT GRANT RESERVE

All capital expenditure (£22,229 in 2005-2006) is financed from HM Governmet Grant. The Grant apportioned is treated in the accounts as a deferred credit. A proportion is transferred annually to the Income and Expenditure Account over the estimated useful life of the assets as Other Income to cover Depreciation.

	2005-06 £	2004-05 £
Balance Brought Forward	11,071	18,241
Apportioned from HM Government Grant	22,229	11,361
	33,300	29,602
Transferred to Income & Expenditure Account	(14,210)	(18,531)
Balance Carried Forward	19,090	11,071

NOTE 4   OTHER OPERATING INCOME

	2005-06	2004-05
	£	£
Transfer from Government Grant Reserve	14,210	18,531
Other	1,946	144
	16,156	18,675

NOTE 5   STAFF COSTS

	2005-06	2004-05
	£	£
Salaries	330,205	307,928
Employer's National Insurance	24,219	22,896
Superannuation	62,877	42,059
Redundancy Costs	-	87,595
	417,301	460,478

5(i)   Average weekly number of full time staff employed
        in the year was   14   15

5(ii)   Employees receiving remuneration over £50,000   0   0

5(iii) Other than the Registrar, none of the Advisory Committee
        members received any remuneration from PLR.

NOTE 6   TANGIBLE FIXED ASSETS

	PLR Computer	Fixtures, Fittings & Equipment	TOTALS
	£	£	£
Cost			
Cost at 1 April 2005	70,379	65,241	135,620
Additions at Cost	22,229	-	22,229
Disposals	(14,905)	-	(14,905)
Cost at 31 March 2006	77,703	65,241	142,944
Depreciation			
Depreciation at 1 April 2005	64,021	60,528	124,549
Charge for 2005-06	10,589	3,621	14,210
Less Charge on Disposals	(14,905)	-	(14,905)
Depreciation at 31 March 2006	59,705	64,149	123,854
Net Book Value at 1 April 2005	6,358	4,713	11,071
Net Book Value at 31 March 2006	17,998	1,092	19,090

The financial effect of revaluing the fixed assets was considered to be immaterial and therefore they have been disclosed at their historic cost value.

NOTE 7   OTHER OPERATING CHARGES

	2005-06	2004-05
	£	£
Administration	137,561	181,321
Accommodation	139,874	114,535
Computer Operating Costs	31,457	42,674
Local Authorities	30,905	31,327
Consultants	17,587	23,614
	357,384	393,471

NOTE 8   OPERATING SURPLUS

		Notes	2005-06 £	2004-05 £
The Operating Surplus of is stated after charging			61,248	1,257
Auditor's remuneration - Audit Fee			16,000	17,625
Operating Leases - Premises Rental		15	109,112	68,391
Travel, Subsistence & Hospitality			17,380	24,031

NOTE 9   PENSION ACCOUNT

This comprises widow's contributions of 1.5% of gross monthly salary deducted from the Registrar's salary.

NOTE 10   DEBTORS

	2005-06 £	2004-05 £
Rent	25,231	23,371
Sundry	2,231	1,587
	27,462	24,958

NOTE 11   CREDITORS:- AMOUNTS FALLING DUE WITHIN ONE YEAR

	2005-06	2004-05
	£	£
Sundry Creditors	18,335	47,195
Corporation Tax	732	1,121
Public Lending Right - Unclaimed & Undistributed:		
99/00	-	4,229
(234 authors) 00/01	7,078	7,207
(236 authors) 01/02	6,987	7,416
(404 authors) 02/03	13,825	14,971
(407 authors) 03/04	15,982	19,386
(481 authors) 04/05	18,222	38,600
(618 authors) 05/06	34,574	-
	115,735	140,125

NOTE 12   PUBLIC LENDING RIGHT RESERVE

	Balance b/f 1.4.05	Transferred from Creditors: PLR Renounced, Returned or Undistributed after 6 years	Public Lending Right Paid	Charge to Income and Expenditure Account	Balance c/f 31.3.06
	£	£	£	£	£
PLR Reserve (a)	9,608	4,179	1,544	-	12,243

(a) The Public Lending Right Reserve is to cover probable further claims for payment of PLR. This is a statutory right enforceable by law - authors have the right to demand payment from the Registrar. Amounts held as creditors and subsequently renounced by authors, or unclaimed and undistributed after six years are transferred to the Reserve. If this is insufficient to meet claims in the year, an appropriation is made from the Income and Expenditure Account. Under the arrangements of the Scheme any unclaimed payments due will lapse after six years. Such amounts are retained in the Reserve for the benefit of authors. The Registrar considers that the Reserve carried forward is sufficient to meet probable claims.

NOTE 13   RECONCILIATION OF OPERATING SURPLUS / DEFICIT TO NET CASH OUTFLOW FROM OPERATING ACTIVITIES

	2005-06	2004-05
	£	£
Operating Surplus	61,248	1,257
Depreciation charge	14,210	18,531
Release from Government Grant Reserve	(14,210)	(18,531)
Decrease/(Increase) in debtors	(2,491)	(7,310)
(Decrease)/Increase in creditors	(24,001)	17,263
Increase in PLR Reserve	2,635	1,848
Net Cash Inflow from Operating Activities	37,391	13,058

NOTE 14   ANALYSIS OF CHANGES IN NET FUNDS

	Year ending 31 March 2006	Year ending 31 March 2005
	£	£
Balance at 1 April 2005	147,808	118,347
Net Cash Inflow	50,512	29,461
Balance at 31 March 2006	198,320	147,808

Net funds comprise only cash at bank and in hand.
There are no bank overdrafts or short-term investments.

NOTE 15   OPERATING LEASES

At 31 March 2006 Public Lending Right had annual commitments under non-cancellable Operating Leases as set out below.

	2005-06	2004-05
	£	£
Operating Leases expiring within:		
One Year	-	-
In the Second to Fifth Years Inclusive	-	-
Over Five Years	93,307	73,044
	93,307	73,044

NOTE 16   CAPITAL COMMITMENTS

At 31 March 2006 there were no capital commitments contracted for, or capital commitments approved but not contracted for (£nil at 31 March 2005).

NOTE 17   NOTIONAL INCOME

Notional return on capital is calculated as 3.5% of average net assets/liabilities for the year and amounts to £2,497 (2004-2005 £772).

NOTE 18   RELATED PARTY TRANSACTIONS

Public Lending Right is a Non-Departmental Public Body (NDPB) sponsored by the Department for Culture, Media and Sport. The DCMS is regarded as a related party. During the year PLR has had various transactions with other Government Departments and public sector bodies which can be summarised as follows:

British Library - provision of bibliographic data

Local authorities - provision of loan sample

None of the members of PLR's Advisory Committee, key managerial staff or other related parties has undertaken any material transactions with PLR during the year.

NOTE 19   PENSIONS

The Government Actuaries Department valued the Registrar's pension liability. As at 31 March 2006, the value of pension liability of the Registrar's scheme was £238,270. GAD assumed a discount rate net of price increases of 2.8% per annum in calculating the pension liability.

The PCSPS is an unfunded multi-employer defined benefit scheme but Public Lending Right is unable to identify its share of the underlying assets and liabilities. A full actuarial valuation was carried out at 31 March 2003. Details can be found in the resource accounts of the Cabinet office; Civil Superannuation (www.civilservice-pensions.gov.uk).

For 2005-06, the employers' contributions of £62,877 were payable to the PCSPS (2004-05 £42,059) at one of four rates in the range 16.2% to 24.6% of pensionable pay, based on salary bands (the rates in 2004-05 were between 12% and 18.5%). Employer contributions are to be reviewed every four years following a full scheme valuation by the Government Actuary. From 2006-07, the salary bands will be revised and the rates will be in a range between 17.1% and 25.5%. The contribution rates are set to meet the cost of benefits accruing during 2005-06 to be paid when the member retires, and not the benefits paid during this period to existing pensioners.

Employees can opt to open a partnership pension account, a stakeholder pension with an employer contribution. No employers' contributions were paid in the year. Employer contributions are age-related and range from 3% to 12.5% of pensionable pay. Employers also match employee contributions up to 3% of pensionable pay. No employer contributions were payable to the PCSPS to cover the cost of the future provision of lump sum death benefits on death in service and ill health retirement of employees.

Contributions due to the partnership pension providers at the balance sheet date were nil. Contributions prepaid at that date were nil.

NOTE 20   FINANCIAL INSTRUMENTS

FRS 13 Derivatives and other financial instruments require disclosure of the role which financial instruments have had during the period in creating or changing the risks that Public Lending Right faces in undertaking its role.

- Liquidity Risks

Public Lending Right's income is derived primarily from grants provided by the Department for Culture, Media and Sport. In 2005-2006, there have been no borrowings, therefore it is believed that Public Lending Right is not exposed to significant liquidity risks.

- Interest Rate Risks

Public Lending Right has no financial liabilities such as bank loans. Cash balances, which are drawn down to pay for operating costs, are held in instant access variable rate bank accounts, which on average carried an interest rate of 2.35% in the year. Public Lending Right consider that the Public Lending Right Central Fund is not exposed to significant interest rate risks.

- Foreign Currency Risks

Public Lending Right holds cash in a variety of bank accounts (UK and foreign). However, despite the dealings in foreign currency, Public Lending Right believes that they are not exposed to any foreign exchange risks, given the small amounts that are involved.

NOTE 21   CORPORATION TAX

Corporation Tax is due on interest received.

	2005-06	2004-05
	£	£
Interest Receivable	13,383	15,199
Interest Received in Year	13,370	15,114
Corporation Tax @ 23.75% on interest received over £10,000 (23.75% in 2004/05)	732	1,121

NOTE 22   POST BALANCE SHEET EVENT

It is the intention to transfer the Registrar's pension into the PCSPC as soon as possible.

Printed in the UK for the Stationery Office limited
on behalf of the Controller of Her Majesty's Stationery Office
5390251   07/06